Beyond Religion

ERIK L. COX

Beyond Religion: Seeing Life from a Kingdom Perspective
Copyright © 2014 by Erik L. Cox

All Rights Reserved: This book is protected by the copyright laws of the United States of America. No part of this book may not be reproduced in any form without permission in writing from the author, except in the case of brief quotations or occasional page copying for personal use or group bible study is permitted and encouraged.

Unless otherwise indicated all Scripture quotations are from the HOLY BIBLE, ENGLISH STANDARD VERSION ® (ESV ®) Copyright© 2001 by Crossway, a publishing ministry of Good News Publishers. All rights reserved. Used by permission

ISBN: 978-0-9913467-0-7
Kingdom Reality Publishing
Detroit, MI. 48201

LETTER FROM THE AUTHOR

"The kingdom of heaven is like treasure hidden in a field, which a man found and covered up. Then in his joy he goes and sells all that he has and buys that field."

– Matthew 13:44

Dear Reader:

By purchasing this book you have just invested in one of the most valuable people in your life – YOU. We all desire to know our purpose – the reason why we were created; and when purpose is discovered it always heightens our sense of self-worth. And so it is within these pages that we will begin to seek purpose; but we will not stop there. As you journey through these pages; we will begin to unearth an element that has been missing from the lives of all those who have surrendered themselves to the ruler-ship of Christ – His Kingdom. Why? Because your purpose is tied to it.

Therefore, this book is not a monetary pursuit. It is more of a personal investment into something far greater than myself – the Kingdom of God. Yes, I do want this book to sale a million copies but only because it will mean a million more people pursuing their purpose. However, I will be equally excited if it sells a single copy and the one who buys it is touched and transformed by the truths inside. Then I have done what I have set out to do.

I must forewarn you that *Beyond Religion* not a religious book and even though it may have been found in the religious section of your local book retailer – that was for shelving purposes only. However, the book, itself, is not intended for anyone looking to push or promote a religious agenda. This book is a guide to one of the most indispensable truths in your life and if you picked it up thinking it might be a good read; know that you have discovered something much greater. This is a map to that *treasure hidden in a field*. This is an exploration of the Kingdom of God. I pray that as you read on, that it speaks to your spirit and unravels your true identity in Christ.

Sincerely your brother in Christ,

Erik L. Cox

Erik L. Cox

DEDICATION

To this generation of believers: May the truths that are hidden inside this work rejuvenate your zeal for the King and as you seek the Kingdom of God, may you obtain the King's heart so that His Love will carry you into His Presence. I pray that while in His Presence you will be able to experience a deeper intimacy with the Creator.

To my children, Samaria (12), Sarai (7), Erik (3) and Kilee (3). You are a constant reminder that my love for the King is constantly on display and that my life must be a living example of His love. I pray that as I continue to seek the King for wisdom and knowledge concerning His Kingdom that it will manifest in your lives as well, thus preparing your hearts to understand your purpose. I love you all with the heart of God that beats within me.

ACKNOWLEDGEMENTS

First and foremost I acknowledge the King of kings and the Lord of lords, Christ Jesus of Nazareth, who faithfully reveals His heart to all who diligently seek Him. I am grateful that He has trusted me with the keys to the Kingdom for the sole purpose of unlocking His truths to His people.

Secondly, I acknowledge my fellow Kingdom brothers, Darrie Williams, Keith Williams and Anthony James. It is their passion for the King that help put me in pursuit of the Kingdom of God and I've been seeking it ever since. Their work in expanding the Kingdom is unparalleled and their love and loyalty for the King is without compromise. I pray that they will always find favor with the King because of the pureness of their heart and the meekness of their spirits.

Last but not least I acknowledge my sister in Christ, Delnita Wadley, who has not only supported the vision for *Beyond Religion* but also shares my passion to take the Kingdom to the nations. I pray that the Father will continue to strengthen her in her purpose and saturate her spirit with kingdom revelation as she prepares for the next phase in her kingdom work.

Table of Contents

Introduction

Part One: Exploring the Kingdom

Chapter One:
Scratching the Surface

Chapter Two:
Digging Deeper into Kingdom

Chapter Three:
Burying Religion

Part Two: Discovering our Purpose

Chapter Four:
Uncovering our Identity

Chapter Five:
Unearthing our Purpose

Chapter Six:
Finding you Faith

INTRODUCTION

EVERYTHING YOU NEED TO KNOW IN ORDER TO WALK IN YOUR PURPOSE IS RIGHT HERE

BEFORE WE GO any further I need you to get this: The entire Bible – all sixty-six books; 1,189 chapters; its nearly 31,173 verses; and its well-over 700,000 words concern two central themes – a King and His Kingdom. Whether you have made your beginning in Genesis or have come upon the Revelation of John, every scripture that you have read is either directly or indirectly related to a King and His Kingdom.

And so as we set out, each of us on our own personal journey of self-discovery, choosing to embrace the concepts introduced in this book will prove to be a paramount decision on your part. Not only will it have a major influence on how you understand God and the Bible, but it will greatly impact your individual purpose as well. But why a King and a Kingdom?

To effectively grasp any concept concerning the Kingdom, we must first recognize that the Bible was never meant to be read or understood as a religious book. It contains within its pages the laws and mandates of a Sovereign King and the rights and privileges extended to those who decide to live under His Kingdom authority. The Bible, then, is the governing influence under which God's people in the earth choose to live. In other words – it is the Constitution of the heaven. And if the Bible is the Constitution of the heaven and we acknowledge heaven as being a type of kingdom, then what exactly is this kingdom? Simply put, the Kingdom of heaven is the government of God and His reign and rule in the lives of His people and on the earth.

"The kingdom is the government of God and His reign and rule in the lives of His people and on the earth."

Now stop reading! You may want to find a pencil, pen, highlighter or even a crayon for the matter and highlight or underline the previous statement. The impact of this statement alone may just change your life. You might not recognize it now but by the end of this book – maybe even after this short introduction – you are going to want to see things from a whole new perspective – and that perspective is a kingdom perspective.

The Kingdom of God has always been God's purpose for man, yet, it has not been until recent years that the Kingdom has become a focal point of our Christian culture. Kingdom is the latest trend to hit the religious sector and it is gaining popularity among every denomination. Our local assemblies have embraced the Kingdom message as if it were some new phenomenon; causing it to sweep through our cultured facilities like a hit new song on the charts – with everyone loving the sound but no one understanding its words. Kingdom has become that song. It is being attached to everything in the church; *kingdom life, kingdom culture, kingdom living, kingdom community,* etc…yet without a clear-cut definition of what the Kingdom really is – it becomes nothing more than a religious fad; an addendum to an already man-made agenda; a counterfeit offer to the religion that he has already offered you.

This is why those of us who have an authentic understanding of kingdom principles and have been entrusted with the keys to unlock the mysteries surrounding the Kingdom of God must begin to *bind* and *loose* according to allotted authority given to us by Christ our King:

> I will give you the keys of the kingdom of heaven, and whatever you bind on earth shall be bound in heaven, and whatever you loose on earth shall be loosed in heaven.
>
> – Matthew 16:19

Sooner or later we will have to confront the religious spirit that has laid claim to everything kingdom and openly waged war against God, His kingdom and His kingdom people. WE ARE UNDER ATTACK!!! Yet our local assemblies – the places set aside to represent the interest of the Kingdom of heaven in the earth –

have become nothing more than breeding grounds that house religious spirits. This has made it possible to revive the pharisaic spirit that Jesus denounced in His day:

> But woe to you, scribes and Pharisees, hypocrites! For you shut the kingdom of heaven in people's faces. For you neither enter yourselves nor allow those who would enter to go in. Woe to you, scribes and Pharisees, hypocrites! For you travel across sea and land to make a single proselyte, and you make him twice as much a child of hell as yourself.
>
> – Matthew 23:13

The Kingdom of God is still being shut in people's faces and the Word of God is constantly being diluted by the doctrine of man. Therefore, if we who have chosen to submit our lives under the original mandate of heaven, hope to advance the Kingdom of God in the earth, then we must be willing to challenge every spirit that has set itself against it – even if means standing against the church.

"The church is not the Kingdom"

The church is not the Kingdom. The church is not even the church, or at least, the church that Christ came to establish. And, if we are to live as God intended for His people to live in the earth, we must expose the religious spirit that has infiltrated the walls of our institutions and penetrated the hearts His people. God wants us free.   ESPECIALLY YOU! Why? Because you have a specific purpose.

And so in this book we will begin removing some of the religious clutter out of our lives and getting rid of those things that prevent us from tapping into our potential and operating in accordance to our purpose. To ensure that we are successful in this endeavor, it becomes necessary to uproot all traces of religion from our lives so that we may break free of the doctrinal teachings of man and become fully operational in the things of God.

As you read on know that everyone desiring to live according to their purpose will be able to do so based upon a biblical understanding of the Kingdom of God. No longer will you have to go through man's recycling bin of religion to discover who you are because your faith will be rooted in the foundational principles of God's word. All you need to know going forward is that your purpose is and always has been tied to the Kingdom of God and in this book the Kingdom will be made real in your life. As we begin to explore the Kingdom of God, we will also have an opportunity to discover who we were created to be. And it is my earnest prayer that your faith will be strengthened and that you will play an instrumental role in pushing the Kingdom forward

Erik L. Cox

Father, as I humble myself before you, I ask that you would forgive this generation of believers. I pray that they will turn their hearts to You and that you will free them from the spirit of religion that has allowed them to live, both foolishly and recklessly before Your throne. I pour out tears of repentance on their behalf – a generation slowly dying due to our disobedience and have yet to realize it. I ask that You will began to breathe new life into them - even if it means my life becoming a martyr for Your glory. I willingly give up me so that Your people may see You. Strip us of the world and of the church so that we might inherit Your kingdom....In Jesus name. Amen!

Part One:
Exploring the Kingdom

CHAPTER ONE:
Uncovering the Kingdom

"From that time Jesus began to preach, saying 'Repent, for the kingdom of heaven is at hand.
– Matthew 4:17

THE MISSION and mandate of Jesus was simple - to restore man back to the Kingdom of God. Now restoration is a word often used in connection with Christianity, yet far too many are ignorant of its actual meaning. Therefore, if the mission of Jesus is to make sense or if it is to have any bearing on our lives then God's plan for restoration must be clearly and concisely understood. To restore can best be defined as the act of reinstating, re-establishing, or returning; it can also mean to repair. With this amplified understanding of restoration let us take a look at the four essential reasons for the coming of Jesus as the Christ.

- To <u>return</u> us back to the Father.
- To <u>repair</u> the relationship that we lost in the garden.
- To <u>re-establish</u> our original purpose in the earth.
- To <u>reinstate</u> our authority over the earth.

To "re" anything denotes an action being done over again, often indicating that it was carried out once before; and so for our purposes we can safely assume that the following are true:

- At one point we were turned toward the Father and lost our way causing us to have to return to Him again;
- We were once paired with the Father and our relationship was lost due to brokenness and now it must be repaired;
- Our purpose in the earth was fully established but at some point we lost sense of ourselves, causing God to have to re-establish in our purpose;
- Our authority in the earth was fully stated at one time but we lost that authority and now must be reinstated in our position.

These are very important factors to keep in mind when considering Jesus' primary objective in the earth. If God's plan was to have man, through the teachings and sacrifice of Jesus, restored back into his original position in the Kingdom; at some point we must acknowledge that the Kingdom is missing from our lives and realize that our return to it is dependent upon us turning back to the God and repairing our broken relationship with Him. We must then start walking in our established purpose and exercising our God-given authority in the earth. Herein are four keys that are essential to unlocking the Kingdom of God in our lives and now that we have them let's open our minds to receive kingdom revelation.

Beyond Religion

WHAT IS THE KINGDOM?

During the introduction of this manuscript it was stated that the Kingdom of God is the government of God and His reign and rule in the lives of His people and in the earth. It should be noted, then, that no claim relating to God or His Kingdom should be made or accepted without the authority of scripture being its main source. Therefore, to authenticate the claim that the Kingdom is the government of God I offer the following verses from the book of Isaiah as a verifying text:

> For unto us a child is born, unto us a son is given: and <u>the government</u> shall be upon his shoulder: and his name shall be called Wonderful, Counselor, The mighty God, The everlasting Father, The Prince of peace. <u>Of the increase of his government</u> and peace there shall be no end, upon the throne of David, and upon <u>his kingdom</u>, to order it, and establish it with judgment and with justice from henceforth even forever. The zeal of the Lord of host will perform this.
>
> - Isaiah 9:6-7

For many of us the above scriptural reference is nothing more than a repeated theme during the Christmas season foretelling the birth of the Messiah.

And while it does, no doubt, prophesy of Jesus' coming – it is more than a birth announcement. This is perhaps one of the most telling passages in all of scripture, in that, it speaks directly to the intent of Jesus and his purpose here in the earth. It also serves as our first piece of objective proof that Jesus never set out to start a religion.

"Jesus never set out to start a religion"

If we can prove with upmost certainty that Jesus never set out to start a religion, not only will be challenging some of the most influential voices in mainstream Christianity, but we will also be forcing ourselves to seek answers to a very potent question, that question being, "What was God's original intent for mankind?"

And if our wanting to know the answer to this question comes from a sincere place, and we thoroughly search the Word for truth; we will find that God's goal for His people in the earth was never religion. It was a government. And so the reason for Jesus coming to the earth was not simply to offer salvation but to establish the government of God – an everlasting kingdom where he [Jesus] would sit on the throne to rule it and establish its judgment and justice.

> Behold, the days are coming, declares the Lord, when I will raise up for David a righteous Branch, and he shall reign as king and deal

wisely, and shall execute justice and righteousness in the land.

- Jeremiah 23:5

And in the days of those kings the God of heaven will set up a kingdom that shall never be destroyed, nor shall the kingdom be left to another people. It shall break in pieces all these kingdoms and bring them to an end, and it shall stand forever.

- Daniel 2:44

These passages are important for two reasons:

1. First they establish Jesus as King and Lord over our lives which means he has complete ownership over us.

2. Secondly, they provide empirical evidence that the religious system which has been allowed to dominate our lives was never God's intention for us – His Kingdom was and still is.

Many of us were exposed to the spirit of religion in the early stages of our spiritual development and consequently it is the only thing we know. The enemy has used this area of our lives to his advantage; allowing us to freely engage in our ritualistic forms of worship, which only keep us in the infantile stages of spiritual growth and hinders us from developing and maturing into the men and women that we were created to be.

But now that we have a clearer understanding of the intent of Jesus – an understanding that cannot simply be tossed aside and rejected by the personal prejudices of our religious suitors; it is imperative that we start releasing ourselves from the religious prison that currently holds us in spiritual captivity. No longer can we accept, embrace, or promote a religious idea of God, but we must seek to know truth so that we can see God as Word the reveals Him to us – as a king overseeing a kingdom. It is only when we adopt this view of God can we began walking in the purpose for which we were created.

"And let them have dominion..."

This is where it all begins and as we dive deeper into our understanding of the Kingdom, the "dominion" factor will be a recurrent theme as it further substantiates the claim that we were never created for a religious purpose. It is for this reason that you and I must desensitize ourselves from the traditions and customs of our current belief system; because if we are going to be effective in our kingdom work, then the Kingdom, itself, must be understood from a biblical perspective. This means uprooting the religious system that has been planted into our lives so that we can successfully accomplish the will of God in the earth. However, this will requires a great deal of faith, a proper understanding of kingdom concepts, and an unwavering commitment to stand on truth.

Beyond Religion

Before we can lay the groundwork for the Kingdom of God, which is the foundational piece of the puzzle as to the reason for our existence, there are some general prerequisites regarding kingdoms that we must familiarize ourselves with. The first thing to note is that a kingdom is different from any other form of governing system. It is a territory where everything within its jurisdiction is influenced by a king. This means that the king owns it all – everything within a king's domain belongs to the king and is under his care and control – including the people. A king cannot be voted into power nor can his power be usurped – it is his birthright. Every word spoken by the king is law and cannot be undone. He is lord of the land and shapes it by his character, his actions, and his words.

These aspects of a kingdom become key when we consider the fact that we are the Kingdom of God – to be shaped and influenced by Christ our King through our obedience and faith so that we might achieve His eternal purpose for us in the earth:

> Now therefore, if you will indeed obey my voice and keep my covenant, you shall be my treasured possession among all peoples, for all the earth is mine; and you shall be to me a kingdom of priest and a holy nation...
>
> - Exodus 19:5-6

This is why Jesus' message of repentance was so vital. By calling man into repentance, Jesus was urging us to turn from our sin so that we could return to the Father and lay claim to the Kingdom that was lost through the disobedience of Adam and Eve. But before we can be completely restored into our rightful place in the Kingdom of God, we must first be released from the spirit of religion that has taken so many of God's people hostage.

The Kingdom of God is not a religious concept and it cannot be offered to us under religious pretenses. As a people placed in the earth with a specific purpose – a purpose that extends beyond the external display of religious piety; it is irresponsible for us to have the only understanding of that purpose dictated to us from man's religious platform. We must choose to seek truth, but the truth that we seek can only be obtained from a thorough examination of the written Word of God. And so it is not enough for us to file into our local assemblies to hear a word from God, only to have the doctrine of the church dominate God's truth. It is essential then, that we stand against the religious system that has been forced into our lives or be found guilty of raping the Kingdom of its value and worth.

**"The Kingdom is not a church idea.
The Kingdom is God's idea."**

The Kingdom is not a church idea. It is God's idea. And because the kingdom is God's idea, it is too big to be contained inside of our religious walls. From the foundations of the world, before anything else that is, was, we were already set aside for God's Kingdom. Our purpose in God has always been connected to His Kingdom, so much so, that it was the focal point of everything Jesus taught in the earth. This is a strong indicator that, if, we hope to live as God intended for His children to live in the earth, the Kingdom must become a priority for us. Jesus states it this way:

> But seek first the kingdom of God and His righteousness, and all these things will be added to you.
>
> – Matthew 6:33

These words of Jesus not only pen the importance of the Kingdom of God but they also tell us the place that it must hold in our lives – the kingdom must come *first*. Yet, the notion of having the Kingdom come first in our lives has been overridden by the majority of sermons scripted from this same verse which point to having *things* added while completely ignoring the significance of simply seeking the Kingdom.

And so to seek anything indicates a diligent search or pursuit of something with the hopes of obtaining or acquiring the particular thing being sought after. By instructing man to seek first the Kingdom of God, Jesus is not simply telling us to look for it, but he wants us to give it priority in our lives so that we may obtain and acquire all the benefits that come along with living under the authority of a King. However, our pursuit and prioritization of the Kingdom means nothing if we are not seeking to live in alignment with its laws and edicts. Therefore, the promise of having everything added is nullified if we are ignorant of what is meant by *"and His righteousness."*

The word righteousness in its Greek connotation is *dikaiosyne`* and it is a governmental term having to do with law. It actually refers to that which is done in agreement with God's standards or to be found in right standing with the Lord after His examination. And so the challenge for everyone who has accepted Jesus as Lord over them is to live in complete alignment with the laws, decrees and edicts of the King. To pursue the Kingdom without being in right standing with the King's law is an empty pursuit altogether. Therefore, if we accept God as our King and acknowledge Him as head of our lives, then we must also accept His Word as our law with the understanding that His law cannot be changed and will not be done away with.

> Do not think that I have come to abolish the Law or the Prophets; I have not come to abolish them but to fulfill them. For truly, I say to you, until heaven and earth pass away, not an iota, not a dot, will pass from

> the Law until all is accomplished. Therefore, whoever <u>relaxes one of the least of these commandments and teaches others to do so will be called the least in the kingdom of heaven,</u> but whoever does them and teaches them will be call great in the kingdom of heaven. For I tell you, <u>unless your righteousness exceeds that of the scribes and Pharisees, you will never enter the kingdom of heaven.</u>
> – Matthew 5:17-20

> Heaven and earth will pass away, but my words will not pass.
> – Matthew 25:24

The above scriptural references are reminders that every word spoken from the mouth of God is relevant and until we start walking in right standing with His word we will never be able to live according to our purpose.

> But he answered, 'It is written, Man shall not live by bread alone, but by every word that comes from the mouth of God.
> – Matthew 4:4

God's words are not only law; but they also contain spirit and life **(John 6:63)**. Yet, the relevancy of this reality has been reduced by the rhetoric of man;

making God's word a nonexistent factor in our lives. And because man has chosen to interpret that which was only meant to be obeyed, the ability to operate in the power given to us at creation has been greatly diminished by the doctrinal teachings of man.

When we consider scripture, we must take into account that it is of God and not of man; meaning that we were never supposed to interpret scripture on God's behalf. We were simply charged with the responsibility of speaking those thing which had already been spoken by God, thereby, reiterating the importance of walking in complete obedience with the laws and precepts already established by the King. The Word of God speaks for itself and it has never been up for private interpretation nor was it ever to be mishandled in the hands of man. God set His word in the earth for one reason and one reason only – to accomplish His will.

> Knowing this first of all that <u>no prophecy of scripture comes from someone's own interpretation.</u> For no prophecy was ever produced by the will of men, but men spoke from God as they were carried along by the Holy Spirit.
>
> – 2 Peter 1:20, 21

> ...so shall my word be that goes out from my mouth; it shall not return to me empty but it shall accomplish

> that which I purpose, and shall succeed in the thing for which I sent it.
>
> – Isaiah 55:10-11

God has exalted His Word above ALL things **(Psalms 138:2)** and because He is a King, it is an act of treason to walk in opposition to the Word that He established in the earth. And so it is a great benefit to us to remain mindful that the words of a king shapes and influences his kingdom and that everyone residing in kingdom territory has the responsibility of living in accordance with the word of the king. Likewise, since God is our Sovereign King, everyone living under His kingdom authority must do according His word or be found in opposition to the throne.

We must take also into account that every form of government has its own set laws – including the Kingdom of God. And whenever a particular law is broken; the one who violated the law loses his or her freedom. In the Kingdom of God it is no different. When we break God's law, through deliberate acts of disobedience, we not only lose the freedom to exercise the rights offered to us as citizens of His Kingdom but we also forfeit the privileges that come along with this Kingdom citizenship.

Citizenship into God's Kingdom is the right of everyone who has been born again (birthed from above) and has confessed Jesus as Lord. Religion has made a mockery of this truth; allowing for its doctrine to eclipse the word of God and allowing tradition to become the trademark of our local assemblies. As a result, people who are genuinely seeking God are limited to the rights and privileges offered by the membership practices of the church, with "kingdom" only being thrown in to make the church's call for membership more appealing. But Jesus did not die for church membership.

"Jesus did not die for church membership"

Jesus' death was to restore us to the Kingdom of His Father and solidify our place as citizens and joint heirs of the Kingdom of God:

> For through him we both have access in one Spirit to the Father. <u>So then you are no longer strangers and aliens, but you are fellow citizens</u> with the saints and members of the household of God.
> – Ephesians 2:19

> <u>Now if we are children, then we are heirs – heirs and co-heirs with Christ</u>, if indeed we share in his sufferings in order that we may also share in his glory.
> – Romans 8:17

Even with this brief description of the kingdom, we have not even begun to scratch the surface of all that the Kingdom of God entails. But now that we have it, let's dive deeper into the Kingdom of God so that we

Beyond Religion

may increase our understanding of God's purpose for our lives.

Erik L. Cox

KINGDOM TRUTHS

- ➤ The mission of Jesus was to restore man back to the Kingdom of God.

- ➤ The Kingdom of God is the government of God and His reign and rule on earth and in the lives of His people.

- ➤ Jesus never set out to start a religion; He came to establish His kingdom.

- ➤ The Kingdom of God is God's governmental reign and rule in the lives of His people and in the earth.

- ➤ Jesus did not die for church membership. His death was to solidify our place in the Kingdom of God.

- ➤ Citizenship into God's kingdom is the right of everyone who has been born again (born from above) and have accepted Jesus as Lord of their lives.

CHAPTER TWO
Digging Deeper into Kingdom

"Where will we turn when our world falls apart and all of the treasures we stored in our barns, can't buy the Kingdom of God?" – Jason Upton

IN THIS BOOK I am trying to plant something of great value into your life and that something is the Kingdom of God. Therefore, if we can agree that the Kingdom of God is a government and not a religion and if you can accept God's governmental reign in your life – then we are ready to move into a greater understanding of kingdom principles.

However, if you are hesitant in your willingness to embrace the concepts introduced thus far, then the remainder of this book will not have the impact needed to change your life. With this in mind, I refuse to move forward without first allowing for a definite understanding of kingdom to flood the lives of all those who desire to live according to their true purpose in the earth. I will plant the seed but it is up to you to accept it as truth.

Beyond Religion is not just another religious paperback trying to proselytize a religious belief. It is more of one man's personal endeavor to promote a truth. And, if, at the presupposition that a truth does exists and if arriving at that truth are common factors in leading man back to the Kingdom of God; then let us begin with the truth at hand:

Erik L. Cox

"The depths of the Kingdom reaches far beyond the confines of our religious beliefs."

The Kingdom of God is not a religious concept nor does it find its origin in the halls of man's own intellect. Because the Kingdom does not originate with man; it must not be watered down with man-made concepts or shaped to fit man's religious agenda. According to Jesus, the Kingdom of God is likened unto a seed. And when this seed is planted into fertile ground, it carries the ability to propel man into the greatness he has been destined for since the beginning of creation. Therefore, we must be certain that we are good ground to sow into so that when the Kingdom seed is planted into our lives we will produce fruit worthy of the King's honor.

> He put another parable before them, saying, 'The kingdom of heaven is like a grain of mustard seed that a man took and sowed in his field. It is the smallest of all seeds, but when it has grown it is larger than all the garden plants and becomes a tree...
>
> - Matthew 13:31-32

God is trying to take us somewhere but, contrary to popular belief, it is not to church. God is moving His chosen people into their purpose and re-establishing them into their rightful position in the earth. In short, He is preparing us for His Kingdom. There is a certain culture that God wants to rise up in the earth but this culture cannot fully manifest until the Kingdom has been properly cultivated into the lives of God's people. And so if we fail in our efforts to gain an accurate depiction of the Kingdom; then we will never be able to produce the culture of heaven in the earth realm. Therefore, we must genuinely seek the Kingdom of God so that we can embrace our original design in the earth.

"Everything we were created to be is tied to the Kingdom of God."

Everything that we are and were created to be is tied to the Kingdom of God. This is why Jesus' entire life was consumed with communicating it truths. The Kingdom of God is such a vital part to who we are created to be that Jesus spent forty days after His resurrection teaching the principles of the Kingdom to the disciples. In essence He was telling them, "You have to get this."

> He presented himself alive to them after his suffering by many proofs, appearing to them during forty days and speaking about the kingdom of God.
>
> - Acts 1:3

Today, the magnitude and importance of the kingdom message has become a trivial matter in the wake of our religious values which are nothing more than an organized set of beliefs, traditions, and customs that try to relate man to an existence of a supernatural power. In a nutshell, religion is man's never-ending search for value and worth – an endless endeavor to make his life more meaningful. But until the Kingdom of God is allowed to supplant religion in our lives, the search for meaning will continue to end in disappointment because religion is not a substitute for the Kingdom of God.

"Religion is not a substitute for the Kingdom of God"

Jesus, himself, never preached a religious message nor did he spend His life promoting the church that he instituted. His main objective in the earth was not to offer us religion but to give us the Kingdom of His Father so that we may live as sons and daughters of God and operate in the authority that comes with being joint heirs to the throne. Our original purpose in the earth begins and ends with the kingdom.

> Fear not, little flock, for it is your Father's good pleasure to give you the kingdom.
>
> – Luke 12:32

Accepting that we have been created for a kingdom purpose is a critical first step in freeing ourselves from religious shackles that we find ourselves in. Of even greater significance, however, is our embracing of kingdom concepts and how we incorporate these values and principles into our own daily lives. And so as we move along, in what could possibly a turning point in how we see ourselves; it will be in our ability to grasp the concepts surrounding the Kingdom that will play a huge part in helping us to define our role and responsibility in the earth – including the call to become the church.

THE ECCLESSIA

One of the most unfortunate occurrences in history has been the translation of the bible from its original Hebrew/Greek form, to the various versions that now cater to our English language. It is due to all of the translations, retranslations, and mistranslations of the original word said to be divinely inspired by God, that the authority of the Bible is constantly being challenged and its authenticity diluted to accommodate our religious associations.

This is particularly true in the case of the church, where the direct result of mistranslated text has led to an influx of religious concepts and ideas. It is these same ideas that keep the truth concerning the Kingdom hidden from us; making the Word of God of no affect in our lives and causing us to walk in complete opposition to commandments of God.

> And he said to them, "Well did Isaiah prophesy of you hypocrites, as it written, "This people honors me with their lips, but their heart is far from me; in vain do they worship me, teaching as doctrines the commandments of men." You leave

> the commandment of God to hold to
> the tradition of men.
>
> — Mark 7:6-8

Now earlier in this work it was stated that the entire Bible is about two things; a King and His Kingdom. If we accept this to be true then we must accept my next statement to be equally true: The church was not established to promote a religious agenda but to achieve the King's purpose. However, because Christianity has allowed for so many conflicting variations of God's Word to be perpetrated as truth; the church which Jesus came to establish has been totally misrepresented in the earth and God's purpose for our lives have been completely misunderstood.

Biblical scholars and linguist (those who studies language), alike, agree that the word church – which finds its origin from the Greek word "ecclesia" – has been misapplied in the context of man's Christianity. Ecclesia, which has its roots dating back to 480 B.C literally means "called out ones" and it was a term applied to the governing body of people assembled together to legislate the affairs of the government in Athens . The Roman Empire later adopted this same model of government as Caesar would convene his council (the ecclesia) together and give them his law. The ecclesia, acting on the authority of Caesar, would take the law and give it to citizens of Rome. And so when Jesus established His ecclesia (the church); he was not starting a religious movement but was instituting a governmental body that would represent the authority of the Kingdom of God in the earth.

"We represent the authority of heaven in the earth."

We will deal with the above truth in subsequent chapters but with the integrity of the church in question and the legitimacy of its authority being challenged; it is important that we carefully consider what the "church" is and identify its role in the earth in relationship to the Kingdom of God. However, if, even the slightest amount of our understanding is predicated on the flawed perspective of our religious beliefs; any attempts to live as the "called out" ones in the earth will be unsuccessful. Therefore, we can no longer operate under the heading of religious institution and expect to be recognized as the authority of God in the earth. It becomes imperative, then, that we make a clear distinction between the ecclesia of Christ and the church that man has resurrected in his name.

MAN'S CHURCH

Now I understand there will always be conflicting viewpoints when it comes to the identity of the church and the place that is should hold in our lives. Even as you fully engage yourselves in this piece of writing, many are unsure of what noun to associate the church with. Religion has taught us to agree with the fact that we are the church, yet, how can we expect the others to accept this claim when the same people who claim to be the church are always on their way to church to have church – leaving many to wonder whether the church is a person, place, or thing.

There was a time when the church was a respected authority in the earth. However, our ability to affect and influence the earth on God's behalf has been negated by our passive acceptance of the role of "religious institution," which has drastically reduced our relevance and rendered us voiceless in matters directly related to the Kingdom of God. Furthermore, because our religious leaders have opted to legally incorporate themselves into this world's governing system,; the church is no longer viewed as valid authority in the earth.

As the Ecclesia of God, we were never at liberty to govern ourselves and by taking that which belonged to God and subjecting it to state law, the church has become nothing more than a government controlled subsidy. And by choosing to become wards of the state under the auspices of our 501C3 status, we have relinquished our role in the earth; trading in our God-given authority simply for the change to be tax exempt. But the true church, the one established by Jesus; it was never meant to become a religious organization. However, by calling forth the church, God was empowering a people to wield authority in the earth.

Beyond Religion

THE TRUE CHURCH

After carefully considering all the reasons for the disconnect between the Kingdom of God and the church, and after playing out every possible scenario as to why the culture of heaven has not yet filled the earth, I have finally come to this conclusion: The culture of heaven has not yet come to the earth because man has not learned how to exercise the power of God in the earth.

When God created man; He gave him dominion. And by giving man dominion, he was instituting man as the sole authority in the earth. But because man [Adam] failed to recognize who he was created to be; the enemy was able to trick him into compromising the position that he was meant to hold in the earth. And so it has been, that, ever since the fall of man; God has been trying to restore us back to our original status in the earth. This alone implies that the coming of Jesus was not simply a means to offer salvation, but by establishing the Ecclesia of God in the earth; another attempt was being made by God to reinsert man back into his role of authority. With that being said, the church in its most general terms, is simply an extension of God's rule in the earth.

"The church is an extension of God's rule in the earth"

But because you and I have been inconsistent in our identification as the church, we have been left impotent in our ability to impact the nations on God's behalf. Therefore, if the church is to once again become a legitimate authority in the earth; its role must be understood from a kingdom perspective and not centered on a bunch of religious traditions or beliefs. And so contrary to the teachings that take place inside of our local assemblies, the church is not the multi-billion dollar enterprise that we find ourselves paying into, in the hopes of finding a God who clearly does not dwell there. It is stated in the book of Acts that God does not dwell in temples made by man and because this statement is a biblical fact; it is irresponsible for anyone claiming to have any knowledge of the Word of God to mislead people into thinking that our structured facilities are even capable of holding the Spirit of the Living God.

> The God who made the world and everything in it, being Lord of heaven and earth, does not live in temples made by man.
>
> – Acts 17:24

You and I must be willing to accept that we are the temple of God – the dwelling place of the Holy Spirit **(1 Cor. 3:16);** and because the Spirit of God dwells in us we have inherited the right to operate in the earth with the full authority of heaven. However, this is not only our right but it also becomes the responsibility of everyone who understands their purpose in the earth. And so the true church – the Ecclesia of God – are those who have been called out of this world's system of governance and have totally submitted themselves under the authority of heaven and the Lordship of our God and His Christ. We are the ones responsible for representing the interest of our King in the earth and, therefore, the charge given to us by the Apostle Paul is as follows:

> ...to bring to light for everyone what is the plan of the mystery hidden for ages in God who created all things, so that through the church the manifold wisdom of God might be now made known to the rulers and authorizes in the heavenly places...
>
> – Ephesians 3:9-10

Herein lies the mission of the church and the role of God's people in the earth; to make known the mysteries of God to the rest of the world. However, to carry this out in an efficient and effective manner, we must first familiarize ourselves with the message that God has been trying to communicate to the world since its foundation – the message that the "Kingdom of God is at hand."

"The mystery of God is the revelation of His Kingdom."

Because the mysteries concerning the Kingdom could not be entrusted to just anyone; God has decided to reveal it to those who have His heart and have committed themselves to living out His purpose in the earth.

> To you has been given the secrets of the kingdom of God, but for those outside everything is in parables so that "they may indeed see but not perceive, and may indeed hear but not understand, lest they should turn and be forgiven.
>
> – Mark 4:11

We all have been set aside for a kingdom purpose and to successfully live out that purpose, it is important that we familiarize ourselves with every aspect of the Kingdom of God and understand that our role is to expand the kingdom in the earth. When God created man, He created him with one specific purpose in mind – to colonize the earth on His [God] behalf and fill it with the culture of the kingdom. Therefore, we must be willing to open ourselves up to receive the revelation concerning the Kingdom so that once it has fully taken root in our lives, we can branch out and take its mysteries the rest of the world.

> And so he said to them, "Go into all the world and proclaim the gospel to the whole.
>
> – Mark 16:15

It is crucial that we understand that there is only one gospel – one message that should be resounding in all the earth. It is the only message that Jesus preached and it is the only message that will turn God's people back to Him. This is the only message that, when preached, can and will move us closer to the reign of God in the earth – we MUST preach the Kingdom!!!

> And this gospel of the kingdom will be proclaimed throughout the whole world as a testimony to all nations, and then the end will come.
>
> – Matthew 24:14

KINGDOM TRUTHS

- The truths concerning God's kingdom goes beyond the confines of religion.

- Religion is nothing more than man's never-ending quest to find some sense of value and worth.

- Everything that we were created to be is tied to the Kingdom of God.

- God wants a certain culture to rise up in the earth, but before the culture of heaven can invade the earth, the Kingdom of God must be properly planted

- The church is an extension of the rule of God in the earth.

- The mission of the church is to make know the mysteries of God and to advance His kingdom in the earth.

CHAPTER THREE
Burying Man's Religion

"See to it that no one takes you captive by philosophy and empty deceit, according to human tradition, according to the elemental spirits of the world, and not according to Christ." – Colossians 2:8

AT THIS POINT we should be ready to move deeper into our understanding of the Kingdom of God, but as we move on, I do not want to be too antagonistic towards the church, because the church is relevant when its purpose is understood. And so as I attempt to dissect the spirit of religion that has somehow influenced how we perceive God, I must be careful not to attack the authenticity of the spirit of God that lives inside the heart of each and every believer.

I am going to assume that most of you are reading this book because you have a genuine desire to know the Father's will for your life. This leaves me with no doubt that your heart for God is real. However, as religion continues to be a dominant part of our culture and we continue to immerse ourselves deeper into its practices; the ability to exercise the power that comes with the revelation of God's Kingdom is thwarted because our understanding of it is built on false truths and misapplied principles.

One of the major faults of religion is: Religion has reduced God to a theology – taking the one thing that should be absolute in our lives and relegating Him down to a study. And because man has been allowed to draw his own conclusions concerning the nature of God; those of us who have a sincere desire to know our purpose in the earth are left to navigate the world's system clinging onto man's idea of God while the truth concerning God remains hidden in His Word.

For too long we have been embedded into man's religious system; programmed to operate under a set of principles and beliefs that have nothing to do with God or His intent for mankind. And so our goal in this endeavor is not to satisfy anyone's craving for more religious jargon but to introduce the Kingdom of God so that we may align ourselves with the will of the King and live according to our purpose. However, if this is to be done successfully, it requires a clearing up of any misunderstanding that we have concerning the Kingdom, while effectively weeding out the misconceptions that have come as a result of religion.

MISCONCEPTION #1: JESUS IS THE FOUNDER OF CHRISTIANITY

Here we have the greatest misconceptions of all time and perhaps the biggest reason why there is such a great divide among God's people in the earth: All of our lives we have been taught that God is the God of Christianity and unless people convert to our "Christian" views and promote our Christian values, then they cannot have access to our "Christian" God.

Beyond Religion

The problem with this mindset is that Christianity is no different than any other religion in the world, with religion itself being man's way of trying to explain a God that he does not quite understand. And so by limiting God's jurisdiction to only include those who classify themselves as "Christians," 4.6 billion people are left to venture in the world with other "gods" or deities and in some cases no god at all.

The fact of the matter is this: God is not the God of Christianity – He is the God of the nations. And as God of the nations He placed man in the earth as a direct replica of Himself so that we could rule on His behalf. God never gave man religion. Man was given purpose and that purpose was to become the embodiment of God in the earth; to exercise authority over it and bring it under our control.

> So God created man in his own image, in the image of God he created him; male and female he created them. And God bless them. And God said to them, 'Be fruitful and multiply and fill the earth and subdue it....
>
> - Genesis 1:27-28

Now our ability to carry out this purpose in its full capacity has been impeded by our passive acceptance of a religious system that has left us incapacitated in our ability to influence the earth. Therefore, if we hope to regain our God-given authority, we must stop hiding behind the cloak of Christianity and began operating in the earth according to the truth.

Jesus did not come into the world to offer it Christianity nor did He intend for man to adopt a set of traditions and customs by which to live. Jesus had one objective and one objective only: To establish the reign of God in the earth and in the heart of man through the pronouncement of the Kingdom. It was God's expectation that once man began to govern himself according to the principles of the kingdom; he would position himself to be reinstated into his rightful place in the earth.

God's goal for mankind has always been that of authority; the first attempt taking place in the Garden of Eden where man was given dominion over the earth. The Hebrew word for dominion is memshalah (mem-shaw-law) and it means "realm" but can also mean "to rule." And by authorizing man to have dominion over the earth, God was giving man a realm (kingdom) to rule in His stead. But when man lost the Kingdom due to disobedience God had to implement a plan of restoration – this time the Kingdom coming through Jesus.

> But he said to them, 'I must preach the good news of the kingdom of God to the other towns as well; for I was sent for this purpose.
>
> - Luke 4:43-44

Beyond Religion

The transfer of the Kingdom and the restoration of authority back to man took place when Jesus spoke these words to the disciples:

> And I confer on you a kingdom, just
> as my Father conferred one on me.
>
> – Luke 22:29, NIV

In the previous chapter it was pre-determined that we were created to be an extension of God's rule in the earth. And so as representatives of the Kingdom we are responsible for advancing its truths, its customs and its culture in the earth realm. Therefore, as I extend the Kingdom to every individual who has the heart to receive it, know that I am not trying to convert you over to Christianity nor am I offering you an invitation to become members of a local "church". Christianity was never God's expectation for your life and neither should it be mine. God's hope for you is that once you receive a proper understanding of His Kingdom and understand who you are in relationship to it; you will be able to walk in your God-given authority given – the authority given to you at the height of creation.

Now I know that many of the themes suggested in this book are not the makings of your traditional Sunday school lesson, but if we hope to wield the power to impact the world on God's behalf, then it becomes mandatory that we start to operate on the basis of truth and not according to the isolated idealisms associated with our religious beliefs. We cannot be so numb to reality that we fail to recognize the faults of our religious system and see how it has singlehandedly corrupted how we perceive God and how we view ourselves.

And so at some point we must be willing to acknowledge that the church as we know it is nothing more than a type of institution – a structured system put in place to get man to adhere to a specific set of organized ideas and beliefs. The problem with this system is that it has isolated us from the original plan of God and forced us to adopt practices and principles that are in direct opposition to His will. But like any group of people who have been integrated into a system for a long period of time; we have been conditioned to uphold the values of the system itself – even when there is a strong indication that the system is failing the people.

Religion is that failing system and God wants us free. God wants this generation released from the religious philosophies and dogma of man that keep us trapped inside of our traditional forms of worship, while leaving us stagnant in our ability to exercise the power of God in the earth. This is why religion has become your enemy's weapon of choice and it has been strategically placed into our lives as a preventative measure to keep us from living out our God-given purpose. But by deciding to embrace the concepts in the book, together we can break free from the bondage of religion and put ourselves in position to push the kingdom forward.

MISCONCEPTION #2: THE ENEMY IS AFTER OUR RELIGION

For many of you the reoccurring theme of kingdom may seem a little too repetitive but let me assure you that understanding its truths WILL save your life. The Word of God clearly states that the people are destroyed due to a lack of knowledge **(Hosea 4:6),** which makes it of great importance for anyone who is operating under the influence of religion to pursue the path of the Kingdom and allow the King to unveil His purpose for your life because, as it is, our religious ways have us headed for destruction.

Now most of us will agree that there is a spiritual war taking place, but what we do not agree on is what is really at stake. Many believe that the strategy of the enemy is to attack the core values of the church and Christianity as a whole, but this is not the case at all. The enemy's assault is aimed directly at you and he is trying to steal, kill, and destroy the kingdom seed that is growing inside of each and every believer. He already knows the value of the Kingdom and the role that it plays in our lives and because it is such a vital part of who we are; he will stop at nothing to keep us from obtaining it:

> When anyone hears the word of the kingdom and does not understand it, the evil one comes and snatches

> away what has been sown in his heart...
>
> – Matthew 13:19

The enemy is not after our religion. He is not trying to spoil any of our man-made traditions nor is he trying to keep us from going to church. His main objective is to stop the advancement of the Kingdom of God in the earth and to keep it from fully manifesting in the lives of God's people. Satan is a strategist and he knows our potential – what we are capable of becoming. He also knows that we are a people who lack the motivation to move toward our purpose. And in order to keep us distracted from God's original plan for our lives, which was for man to rule and have dominion over the earth; he [Satan] willingly concedes to our religious ways; knowing that they are nothing but empty gestures before a real God and that the truth concerning the Kingdom will never be found inside of the walls of man's religious infrastructure.

The goal of the adversary is to keep the Kingdom from becoming real in our lives because he knows once our potential collides with our purpose, change will no longer be just an idea; it will become our pursuit. Therefore, this generation of people must make a conscious decision to understand their potential and start living according to purpose, because the ability to impact nations is in our grasp. This is why I chose to write *Beyond Religion* at such a critical time – the people of God need to see something different taking place in the earth. With the world's governing system displaying a strong inability to protect the basic freedoms of its citizens and our religious institutions failing to demonstrate the "power" that supposedly comes with their teachings and beliefs; people are starting to question the stability of both systems and are looking for something more secure.

For almost as long as the world has been in existence; man has taken his idea of God, blended it with the various traditions of other cultures and concocted religion as a means of trying to explain the unexplainable. And so rather it be in our tragedies or our triumphs; our victories or defeats; our successes or our failures; we associate every detail of our lives to our strict adherence to the rituals that accompany our particular beliefs with little or no regard to whether or not these ideas are truly in alignment with the will of God.

Sadly, in today's culture, it is the rituals that are being held in higher esteem than God; causing many to act independent of Him and allowing man to insert institutionalized religion as his solution to the plethora of problems facing humanity. And so it goes: Marital problems? Come to church. Lost your job? Come to church. Homeless? Come to church. Diagnosed with cancer? Come to church. And so Sunday after Sunday millions upon millions pile into local assemblies all over the world hoping to overcome some of life's most difficult circumstances – only to be sent away on an emotional high but never receiving the power they came desperately searching for. It is because the church has proven to be incompetent in its ability to impact the lives of the God's people that so many are choosing to simply adapt to what is going on around them instead of exercising the power of God and rising above it all.

"We settle for conformity because we have yet to see an authentic display of God's power take place in our lives and in the earth."

This is the reason why I cannot write to protect the image of the church – because the church is not reflecting the image of God. And until the church becomes a direct reflection of God in the earth; it is and will continue to be an irrelevant factor in the lives of God's people. This means that one of the goals for man in the earth must be the restoration of the *Imago Dei* (Latin; image of God) in the earth. But in order for this to happen, our buildings can no longer serve as dens of entertainment, but must become embassies of truth; faithful in its representation of the Father and the establishment of kingdom principles in the lives of His people.

With everything that is taking place in the world today; there is a people who need to know that there is still hope. However, this hope that I speak of cannot be in some distant "god" who dwells in the highest heaven with no regard for his own creation. Therefore, we must put our faith in an ever-present God; one who not only created man in His image but poured a portion of Himself into the man that He created so that we could operate in the earth as He operates in heaven. Therefore, the power to change the very conditions that we live in lies in our willingness to grab hold of who we were created to be.

There is a shifting taking place in the atmosphere and there has been a shaking of the earth's core which has awakened a generation to truth. As a result, a people have risen up in the earth – a people who have stripped themselves of titles, doctrine, and their dependence on man's religious system in order to carry out the original mandate for mankind – AUTHORITY! These are those who have decided to break free from the chains of religious bondage in order to operate in what religion itself has failed to provide – TRUTH!!!

This is why the church – as an institution – can no longer be looked to as a viable authority in the earth; because the church is no longer operating in the authority of God. The influx of religious ideas into the walls of our structured facilities has made it possible for man to freely speak into our lives on without hesitation or interference. The concern should be, that, since much of what man believes about God stems from a theoretical study of His

Word; most of his views concerning the nature of God are founded upon his own theology and have nothing to do with the Word of God. Consequently, opportunistic men have been allowed to force their personal agendas into the lives of God's people with little or no regard for scripture; and when a single idea is used to control or manipulate an entire group of people, it can no longer be considered religious freedom, but now becomes a form of systematic oppression.

"When a single idea is used to control or manipulate an entire group of people…that idea becomes a form of systematic oppression."

We, the people of God, have indeed become systematically oppressed by the unfounded principles of organized religion. And because we blindly accept every concept that has the name of Jesus attached to it; we now find ourselves enslaved in our own belief system. Darrie Williams, my brother and colleague in the joint effort to expand the Kingdom of God to the earth; he once said to me that religion is the only system in which people are given answers without ever questioning the answers they are given. This statement alone was the turning point in my spiritual journey and it opened my eyes to the need of God's people - the need to break free from the system of religion.

However, before we can procure any type of spiritual freedom and break free from the chains of religious enslavement; we must first be willing to confront the religious system itself. Because, if any system is to be changed, then the ideas upholding that particular system must be challenged. And so while most of the leaders of this generation are calling for, yet, another spiritual revival – not realizing what spirits they are causing to rise up in the earth; I opt for a spiritual revolution – a breaking away from every religious concept and idea that is in direct violation to the Word of God. It is only when we start challenge everything that has been put in front of us, do we give ourselves the best chance to arrive at a truth.

And so it goes without saying that we can no longer allow a single man to serve as the mouthpiece of a God in our lives, especially, when there is no real assurance that his words are in alignment with the will of God. And if we accept all of man's answers without ever questioning his motives, we position ourselves to be manipulated by the same system that we are trying to escape. Therefore, it is our responsibility to make sure that any instruction that we receive is from our personal study of God's Word and from man's personal views.

As a representative of the Kingdom of God, man was never permitted to speak on his own accord when it concerned the Word of God. We were only supposed to speak those things already spoken by the King. Even Jesus was careful not to communicate his own ideas; but made certain that every word that proceeded from his mouth was in alignment with the will of God

> Jesus answered, "My teaching is not my own. It comes from the one who sent me.
> – John 7:16, NIV

With this in mind I cannot, in good conscious, offer you the regurgitated themes of man's religious beliefs and expect you to find God in them. And so if you to truly want to find God for yourself, you must be brave enough to lay aside the recycled pathologies handed down to you by religion's past predecessors and be willing to embark upon a personal journey of self-discovery that will lead you directly into His truths. Because if God is to truly exist in YOUR life, He cannot simply exist because man says He does. The existence of God must be predicated on the fact that "GOD IS."

"If God is to exist in our lives, He cannot exist simply because man says He exist."

As an infinite being, having no boundaries or limits, the true essence of God cannot be explained by the finite minds of man. And yet, the closest evidence that we have which proves the existence of the Creator is the creation itself. This is a strong indicator that if we hope to find God, He cannot be handed down to us from our religious platforms. The search for God must begin deep within ourselves and once we identify who we are according to His Word; we

Beyond Religion

will find that God resides in each of us and that we were called to be "god" in the earth.

> I have said, "You are gods; and all of you are children of the most High.
>
> – Psalms 82:6

Many theologians and pastors of the Christian faith will refute the claim that the search for God begins within you. They fear that the claim itself questions the credibility of everything taught in the church and that it will lead many outside of the church to search for their identity in God. But if scripture is our sole source of authority then we must take heed to what it says and it states::

> And I will give you a new heart, and a new spirit will I put within you. And I will remove the heart of stone from your flesh and give you a heart of flesh. <u>And I will put my Spirit within you</u> and cause you to walk in my statutes and be careful to obey my rules."
>
> – Ezekiel 36:26

From the onset my purpose has been clear – to free God's people from the religious fetters that keep us in unnecessary spiritual bondage. Therefore, I urge you to stop seeking God inside of the context of Christianity and let the search for God begin inside of you. If we continue to limit an omnipresent God to the confines of our brick and mortar; our truth concerning Him will always be centered on someone else's principles.

And so it is not my intent to offer you anything that I say as a self-proclaimed truth. I simply want to share with you my biblical findings and offer knowledge, so that as you take this journey can arrive at your own truth. Therefore I encourage all of you reading, to reject everything that has ever been taught to you and be open to knowledge so that you may establish your own truth.

If at any time we can't challenge our belief system and at the end of the day, still believe what we believe, then we have not yet arrived at truth. So we must seek an understanding of God for ourselves and as we move on to the discovery of who we are, don't be afraid to embrace your true nature. It is only when we discover truth for ourselves that we will be able to remain steadfast and immovable in our faith and accept who we were called to be.

Beyond Religion

KINGDOM TRUTHS

- As religion continues to be a dominant part of our culture and we continue to immerse ourselves deeper into its practices; our ability to exercise the power that comes with the revelation of the Kingdom.

- God never gave man religion; man was given purpose and that purpose was to become the embodiment of God in the earth; to exercise authority over it and bring it under his control.

- As representatives of the Kingdom of God, we are responsible for advancing its customs and culture in the earth.

- Satan's main objective is not try and spoil any of our traditions or customs nor is keep us from going to church. His goal is to stop the advancement of the Kingdom of God in the earth and to keep it from fully manifesting in the lives of God's people.

- The existence of God cannot be predicated on the theories of man, and so if God is to exist in our lives, He must exist simply because He is and for no other reason.

Part Two:
Discovering Your Purpose

CHAPTER FOUR
Uncovering your Identity

> "When I look at your heaven, the work of your fingers, the moon and the stars that you have set in place, what is man that you are mindful of him, and the son of man that you care for him? – Psalms 8:3-4

ALL OF OUR LIVES we search for a sense of relevancy; constantly pursuing the possibility that there is more to us than what meets the natural eye. But because every attempt to identify with our true nature has constantly ended in failure; many have chosen to hide themselves in the shadows of religion in the hopes of having their feelings of inadequacies satisfied by man's idea of fulfilment. But what happens when man's religion is no longer capable of containing your craving to know who you are and who you were created to be? Now I don't want you to be alarmed by these questions because I, too, asked myself the same things and this is where my story begins.

"There has to be more to me than this." I know that many of you turning these pages can sympathize with these words, seeing that, we all have felt this way at some point in our lives. And so these were my exact thoughts as I sat through another Sunday morning service unfulfilled. As always, the choir was fully engaged in its traditional march up song, "I'm Glad to be in the Service," but honestly speaking, I was not too thrilled to be there. I had been attending church all of my life but no matter how much I sought closeness with the Father, it always felt like He was far away. Still, I carried on with the ritual of waking up every Sunday morning hoping to find God in the one place where everyone said He dwelt – yet He never seemed to be there on the Sundays I attended.

But there I was, waiting on God to reveal Himself. He had to be there. I needed Him to be there. Because while everyone else carried on with their rehearsed worship, I sat silently, questioning my faith: What was this all for? What was the purpose of church? What was the point of preaching? What was the reason for me? It was at that moment when I decided to leave the church altogether in order to seek this thing called the Kingdom of God.

This might be a good place to mention that I was ministering at the time. I had been preaching a little over eleven years and if I may say so myself, "I was pretty good at it." I was well-trained in the ways of Baptist tradition and I possessed an uncanny ability to articulate things that I wanted others to believe. I would faithfully rehearse my scripted sermons over and over in the mirror, and when it came time to stand behind that "sacred" desk, I eloquently spoke on things I did not understand. I led many people to church, but they were no closer to God or His Kingdom than they had been before. It wasn't until I became consumed with the Kingdom for myself that I realized what I had become. I was nothing more than a robot programmed to operate inside of a religious system and for the first time in my life I longed to be free.

Whether we choose to acknowledge it or not, religion is a dangerous thing – especially when fueled by man's need to be seen as relevant. Religion, itself, is birthed out of the Pharisaic spirit that ruled Jesus' day; whose own desire to be seen as relevant led them to seek their own glory; often times with a blatant disregard for God's will. And because we, just like the Pharisees of that day, place such a high view on our religious practices with a limited understanding of God's word; it is the practices themselves that have become one of the leading causes for much of the skepticism surrounding the existence of God. Even those of us who absolutely believe that God does exist; because we only see Him from a religious perspective; the perception that we have of Him has been greatly misconstrued.

In reality, religion is the reason why many in the world today are conflicted about who God is. It is the reason why thirty-three percent of the world's population is Christian; twenty-one percent Muslim; thirteen percent Hindu; and another thirteen percent either atheist or non-believers. Religion is the reason why men strap themselves to bombs and sacrifice their lives in the name of their "god" and it is responsible for millions and millions of deaths – six million at the hands of "Christians" alone. And here is the dagger for those who believe that Jesus is the Christ...

"Religion is what killed Jesus"

Now there are many who started out on this journey with us, who, because of my last statement are going to put this book down. Instead of opening their mind's to either accept or reject this as a truth; they will automatically write it off as a blasphemous lie from the pit of hell because it is contrary to what has already been rooted in them through the doctrinal teachings of man. And because man's doctrine has been allowed to govern our belief system; it alone dictates what we believe about God and how we believe it. As a result we are programmed by default to reject any idea that does not agree with our religious philosophies or pulpit principles – even if those ideas do hold biblical truth.

And so I commend all of you who courageously turn the pages of this book knowing that the content inside challenges the very concepts that you have been taught about God. However, it is not my intent or the intent behind this book to have anyone question their faith in God. On the contrary, my hope is that, as you read on, you will develop a deeper understanding of who you were created to be and that your overall faith in God can be strengthened. The expected outcome is that once you embrace who you are and what you were placed in the earth to do, that you will take up the mantle of authority given to you at creation and begin operating in the earth in the full power of God.

But before we can get to this point in our journey – the part we walk in the power of God; we must understand that we were never created for religion and that religion is nothing more than man's futile attempt to make himself relevant in the eyes of God and other men. This is the reason why we covet titles, embrace traditions, and participate in ritualistic forms of worship – because these are the things that make us feel important. But to truly appreciate who we were created to be, we must be willing to empty ourselves of all traces of religion; because deep down in the recesses of the soul, buried beneath the rubble of our broken traditions and church doctrine, lies the person you were created to be. And for the remainder of this chapter we will begin to unravel that person so that you can discover the "real" you.

THE IMAGE OF GOD

The first thing we need to know concerning ourselves is that we are more than we give ourselves credit for being. This statement alone is a difficult one to grasp, seeing that, many have grown up in an era of Christianity where the "sinner saved by grace" mentality is the norm; making it acceptable for a man to tolerate the sin nature without ever seeking to live righteously before a Holy God. One of God's direct commands to mankind was to "be ye holy for I am holy," which implies that the ultimate goal for humanity is to be like God in the earth. But if we are to achieve this higher standard of living, it requires us to reject our lower levels of thinking; and when we acquiesce and silently submit to the "sinner saved by grace" labeling as an aspect of who we are; we are in fact crippling ourselves from becoming what we were created to be.

Therefore we must learn to boldly accept that we are, indeed, the resemblance of God, predestined to reflect His glory in the earth. This was God's original design for us but ever since the fall of Adam and Eve, man has struggled to identify with this part of who he is:

> Then God said, '<u>Let us make man in our image, after our likeness.</u> And let them have dominion over the fish of the sea and over the birds of the heavens and over the livestock and over all the earth and over every creeping thing that creep on the earth.' <u>So God created man in His own image,</u> in the image of God he created him; male and female he created them.
>
> – Genesis 1:26-27

You and I were created in the image and likeness of God for the purpose of exercising dominion in the earth. This has always been God's intent for mankind and by decreeing into the atmosphere, "Let them have dominion," God was instituting man as the sole authority in the earth, thereby, giving us the legal license to rule the earth as He rules heaven. This position, however, was forfeited when man failed to exercise authority over the serpent.

> Now the serpent was more crafty than any other beast of the field that the Lord God had made. He said to the woman, 'Did God actually say, "You shall not eat of any tree in the garden?' And the woman said to the serpent, 'We may eat of the fruit of the trees in the garden, but God said, "You shall not eat of the fruit of the tree that is in the midst of the garden, neither shall you touch it, lest you die.' But the serpent said to the woman, 'You will not surely die. For God knows that when you eat of it your eyes will be opened, and you will be like God, knowing good and evil."
>
> – Genesis 3:1-5

Revisiting the encounter between Eve and the serpent and understanding what actually took place between the two in the garden is essential, especially, if we hope to regain what we loss at the hands of the serpent. It is necessary, then, that we focus on two major points of emphasis that need to be expounded if we are to ever overcome the impact of the garden experience – the first point being Eve's knowledge of God's Word.

When Eve was questioned by the serpent concerning God's instructions at creation; she was able to effectively communicate every word that God had spoken to Adam, which is a stronger indicator that her knowledge of God's word was never a problem. However, the issue for Eve came when, not knowing who she was, left her vulnerable to the craftiness and cunningness of the serpent. So let's consider the asking price for her disobedience to God's word.

> But the serpent said to the woman, 'You will not surely die. For God knows that when you eat of it your eyes will be opened, and you will be like God…

Now as we take a closer look at this passage we see that the serpent did not offer Eve anything that she had not already been given. Eve was already created to be like God – it was already part of her genetic makeup. But because she did not know her own worth and failed to identify with her "god-like" nature, the serpent was able to convince her to prostitute her value; making it easy for him to pimp her out of paradise. This leads me to my second point and point simply suggests to us that knowing God's Word is not enough.

"Knowing God's Word is not enough"

There are a countless number of believers who truly know the Word of God. They are well-versed in scripture and can quote the bible forward and backwards. However, when it comes to incorporating biblical principles into their own lives, these same individuals are unable to do so because they have not yet adopted the nature of God, which makes it safe to conclude that knowing God's Word means nothing if we fail to identify with His nature.

"Knowing His Word means nothing if we fail to identify with His nature."

To know the Word of God without identifying with the nature of God is like having the manual to an entertainment system that did not come with all the parts. No matter how we try to operate the system it will fail to function properly because it is missing a key component to what makes it what it is. Likewise, we cannot function in the power that is God, if who God is, does not become part of who we are.

THE NATURE OF GOD

Going forward, the nature of God and how it coincides with the culture of the Kingdom will be a continuous area of concentration as we try to arrive at some at some kind of consensus as to who we are. And while I do not want to discourage anyone from continuing on with this journey; the fact remains that not everyone reading will be able to grasp the concepts that are inside.

> Then the disciples came and said to him, 'Why do you speak to them in parables?' And he answered them, 'To you it has been given to know the secrets of the kingdom of heaven, but to them it has not been given.
>
> – Matthew 13:11-12

The good news in all of this is that your ability to embrace the concepts within this work, but more importantly, those of the bible is solely dependent on you. God is looking for a people who want His heart – a people unafraid to press into His presence and completely surrender their lives to Him. His own word offers confirmation that when we seek Him with all of our heart, he will be found among us; making it mandatory for us to turn our hearts toward the Father, so that He may reveal Himself to us.

> But from there you will seek the Lord your God, and you will find Him if you search for Him with all your heart and all your soul.
>
> – Deuteronomy 4:29

> For I know the plans I have for you, declares the Lord, plans for welfare and not for evil, to give you a future and a hope. Then you will call upon me and come and pray to me, and I will hear you. You will seek me and I will find me, when you seek me with

Beyond Religion

all your heart.

– Jeremiah 29:11-13

If we truly want to know God in His fullness, we must be willing to completely open up to Him. This means giving Him access to every part of our lives, including those broken areas, so that He can start picking up the fragmented pieces and once again, mold us into His image and likeness. Therefore, total surrender is a MUST for all who hope to have the presence of God poured into their individual persons, which makes the goal towards which all of our efforts should be directed that of personal intimacy. And because our identities are completely wrapped in God, every experience we have with Him must be real.

"Every experience with God must be real"

If intimacy with God is the goal of His people in the earth; then we cannot have that experience dictated to us by the hierarchy of religious thought. It is because religion has already become such a prevalent thing among us that we adapted so many versions of truth, with truth being any set of ideas or belief that we willingly accept, promote, or embrace as our own. The problem with these self-proclaimed "truths" is they are not really our own, but are the perceived realities of someone else's beliefs. And so when it comes to our understanding of God, we do not possess an authentic view of Him; we have simply adopted the values of others and embraced them as our own.

This sad occurrence has left many to operate in the earth with a plagiarized view of God – one that has been copied verbatim from the religious concepts handed down to us by man. And because these ideas have been embedded into our way of thinking; we often times try to force them onto others and pass them off as truth. But any idea that we perceive to be true, that is not based on knowledge, is not a truth at all – it is ignorance. So before we embrace any concept of God; we must first seek knowledge of God – knowledge that can only be authenticated by the Spirit of God.

> But the Helper, the Holy Spirit, whom the Father will send in My name, He will teach you all things, and bring to your remembrance all that you I said to you.
>
> – John 14:26

It is not up to me or anyone else to offer you our personal views on God. We are to simply supply you with knowledge so that you can decipher through all that has been offer to you and arrive at your own truth. But if you fail to challenge everything that is offered to you and naively accept it all as true; then you allow someone else's opinion to become your only form of truth. And so it is important that we recognize that God is not a respecter of persons and

Beyond Religion

that He will reveal Himself to every heart who has a desire to know Him. Furthermore, there is no special anointing given to anyone that God has not made available to everyone and once we have subjected ourselves under the anointing of His Spirit, we will no longer be a need to be taught by man because the Spirit of God, that dwells in us, will teach us ALL things.

> But the anointing that you received from him abides in you, and you have no need that anyone should teach you. But as his anointing teaches you about everything, and is true, and is no lie – just as it has taught you, abide in him.
>
> – 1 John 2:27

One of the biggest flaws of man is our inability to admit when we are wrong or simply don't know a thing. However, rather than to acknowledge when we are unsure about something; we are more likely to give you our personal views concerning the matter and leave you at the mercy of our misunderstanding. And so when it concerns the will of God's for our lives, we must reduce our dependency on man and learn to trust in the Spirit of God that dwells inside of us.

As we move further along in this attempt to discover our true selves, I will be the first to admit that I do not know everything there is to know concerning our spirituality. My prayer is that as you seek truth, the Spirit of God will direct you in all things concerning God and that Beyond Religion will serve only as a guide to help point you into God's direction. I can assure you that I have not been given any special knowledge concerning the things of God but like Paul I can also say with certainty that the gospel that speak is not man's gospel. I did not receive it from any man nor was I taught it but is it has been revealed to be through the revelation of Jesus Christ **(Galatians 1:11-12).**

Therefore, if any of these words that I write agree with your spirit in any way, shape, or form; it is only because your spirit desires to do the will of the Father. I speak nothing of my own accord; but am simply a vessel who has been emptied before the Lord for His purpose.

> So Jesus answered them, "My teaching is not my own but his who sent me. <u>If anyone's will is to do God's will he will know whether the teaching is God or whether I am speaking on my own authority.</u>
>
> – John 7:16-18

I do not seek my own glory in any of this. I simply want people to know God and how He ties in to their purpose. But the ONLY way to know God is to allow His Spirit to connect with your spirit. With this in mind, let's try to answer the question "Who is God?"

Beyond Religion

GOD AS FATHER

Throughout the bible there is one idea that is made quite clear and this idea allows us to relate to God as our Father. The Apostle Paul expresses this in his first letter to Corinth and later reiterates the same idea in the book of Ephesians:

> Yet for us there is one God, the Father, from whom all things and for whom we exist, and one Lord, Jesus Christ, through whom are all things and through who we exist.
>
> – I Corinthians 8:6

> There is one body and one Spirit – just as you were called to the one hope that belongs to your call – one Lord, one faith, one baptism, <u>one God and Father of all</u>, who is over all and through all and in all.
>
> – Ephesians 4:6

Even Jesus, when teaching what many have come to know as the Lord's prayer, encouraged us to start our prayers by acknowledging God as "Our Father."

> After this manner therefore pray ye:
> <u>Our Father</u> which art in heaven,
> Hallowed be thy name.
>
> – Matthew 6:9

It is easy to embrace the concept of God being our Father, especially, when it allows us to identify with

His loving nature. We rely on God to be this loving father and often point towards His love every time we find ourselves walking outside of the framework of His design. And even though God has made His love available to us on a daily basis, we have a tendency to abuse the privilege of being called sons and daughters of God because we don't understand what it truly means to have Him as a Father. As a result, we have completely squandered the role that we were predestined to fill in the earth since the epitome its creation.

> I have said, Ye are gods; and all of
> you are children of the Most High.
>
> – Psalms 82:6

If God is truly our Father then we must learn to walk as children of the Most High. By creating man in His image and giving him dominion in the earth; God was calling forth sons and daughters who would inherit ruler-ship not religion. As sons and daughters we have been designated to cause the earth resemble heaven. This was the same directive given to Adam and Eve at creation and though they were unable to fulfil this task due to their disobedience; God's goal of having children who would exercise dominion in the earth has never changed. Simply put, you were destined to dominate.

GOD AS KING

While it is important for us to recognize God as our

Father; it is equally important that we acknowledge Him as King.

> For the Lord is a great God, and a great King above all gods.
>
> – Psalms 95:3

David, a king in his own right, understood the importance of honoring and respecting God as King and in Psalms 47, he acknowledged the kingship of God and His reign over the earth:

> Clap your hands, all peoples! Shout to God with loud songs of joy! For the Lord, the Most High, is to be feared, <u>a great king over all the earth.</u> He subdued peoples under us and nations under our feet. He chose our heritage for us, the pride of Jacob who he loves. Selah. God has gone up with a shout, the Lord with the sound of a trumpet. Sing praises to God, sing praises! Sing praises to our King, sing praises! <u>For God is the King of all the earth</u>; sing praises with psalm! <u>God reigns over the nations</u>; God sits on his holy throne.
>
> – Psalms 47:1-8

But because this generation has failed to recognize the kingly authority of God, which has been passed to us as joint heirs with Christ, we have been left vulnerable to a religious system that has asserted dominance over us through its own doctrinal teachings. And as long as the Kingdom remains a foreign concept to us, we will continue to subject ourselves to peasant-like conditions when royalty is ours by design. We are royalty – it is in our DNA. But until we start seeing ourselves as such, we will continue to be ineffective in our purpose.

We must be remember that because God is our Father we enjoy the privilege of being called sons and daughters. But because our Father is also King we bear the responsibility of walking in complete obedience to His decrees and statutes (His Word) while rightfully claiming our place as joint heirs to His throne.

> The Spirit himself bears witness with our spirit that we are children of God, and if children, then heirs – heirs of God and fellow heirs of God and fellow heirs with Christ, provided that we suffer with him in order that we may also be glorified with him.
>
> – Romans 8:16-17

You are royalty. Yes, I said it again, "You are royalty." But even now most of you are afraid to walk in what you were created to be. You are intimidated by the idea of taking on the persona of God and becoming a reflection of Him in the earth. This, in part, is due to our limited understanding of kingdom principles which has left us stifled in our ability to operate in the earth as God's operates in heaven.

For too long we have identified ourselves from a religious perspective, only seeing ourselves from someone else's point of view and completely missing out on who we were created to be. To reclaim our identity we must choose to see ourselves for who we are and not what religion has trained us to be. We are were created for a Kingdom purpose – to rule and influence earth on behalf of heaven. Royalty! This is who we are. This is who we were created to be. We are the sons and daughters of God in the earth.

Erik L. Cox

KINGDOM TRUTHS

- Religion is a dangerous thing, especially when it is fueled by man's need to be seen as relevant.

- We were never created for religion and religion itself is nothing more than man's futile attempt to make himself relevant in the eyes of God and other men.

- The ultimate goal for humanity is to be like God in the earth but in order for us achieve this higher standard of living requires a breaking away from our lower levels of thinking.

- To truly get to know God in His fullness we must be willing to surrender every area of brokenness that accompanies our lives over to Him.

- To reclaim our identities, we must choose to see ourselves for who we truly are and not for who religion has trained us to be. We were ROYALTY!

CHAPTER FIVE
Unearthing Your Purpose

"The whole world awaits you, so why limit yourself to their little box? You are so much more than you ever imagined, so whatever you are thinking...think BIGGER!" - Erik L. Cox

NOW THAT WE have uncovered our identities, let's move right into our purpose. The Kingdom has always been God's plan for you. Accept it. Before the foundations of the world were laid, while man was still in the embryonic stage of his existence – conceived in the mind of God but not yet birthed by the breath of God – our reason for being was Kingdom. And while the rest of the world still searches for a sense of relevancy; God had already chosen you for a far greater purpose. He chose you for the advancement of His Kingdom.

Until now, many of you have had no desire to pursue your purpose. Your patience and passion to pursue that which you were created for has constantly been disrupted by the church's persistence that we are nothing but "filthy rags." And so in an effort to satisfy the status quo of Christianity, we have isolated ourselves in the earth, completely giving up our right of authority for fear of not measuring up to the church's standards. But I say to you that you are more than what they have said about you and contrary to what is taught from man's pulpit, the

Kingdom is your birthright and it has been since the foundations of the earth:

> Then the King will say to those on his right, "Come, you who are blessed of My Father, inherit the kingdom prepared for you from the foundation of the world."
>
> – Matthew 25:34

From the beginning of time you and I were purposed to expand the Kingdom of God so that the culture of heaven would invade the earth realm through us. And so when the God of the heavens took the dust of the earth and formed man in His image and likeness, He was preparing man for dominion over the earth.

> Then God said, "Let us make man in our image, after our likeness. And let them have dominion...
>
> - Genesis 1:26

This is the reason why the words, "let them have dominion" seem to resonate in our spirit every time we hear them; it is what we were purposed for in the earth. To dominate or to be given dominion, in general terms, is to be given the right to control, govern, or rule by superior authority. So by allowing man to have dominion in the earth, God was giving his sons and daughters territory to rule, govern, and bring under our control. In essence He was saying to man, "Be me in the earth and rule the earth as I rule heaven."

Beyond Religion

Now this is a powerful truth that has laid dormant in wake of our religious traditions and beliefs. And because religion is such an intrusive force in our lives and the culture that surrounds us; it continues to rob us of who we are. Furthermore, because we don't know what we were predestined to be, we have been reduced to mere puppets awaiting the next opportunity to perform on man's religious stage. As a result, our worship of God has become rehearsed – nothing more than a song and dance show that we put on to appease the "god" of our religion.

PURPOSED FOR WORSHIP

It is kind of funny when you think about: All of our lives we've had this tendency to poke fun at the indigenous people of ancient civilizations who worshipped their "gods" by dancing half-naked around barn fires while singing songs in their native tongue. We laugh and write this behavior off as "pagan," but when you think about it, are we really any different? Every Sunday we enter our local assemblies dressed in our Sunday's best, only to take part in ritualistic "worship" practices that that include us dancing in our "sacred" sanctuaries, while singing songs of praise in an unknown tongues. And so our "worship" of God is no different than the ancient cultures of the world, with the only distinguishing factor being the three-piece suit.

The sad thing about these behavior patterns, which have become synonymous with "Christian" worship, is that the behavior, itself, is inconsistent with the biblical expression of worship. And by continuing to offer God rehearsed songs and dances as reasonable acts of worship; we have reduce ourselves to nothing more than jesters performing in the King's court. So it goes without saying that, though we are purposed for worship; we must strongly consider what we offer to God as such. If all we have to offer God is the redundancy of our ritualistic practices but fall short in our efforts to offer Him our obedience, then our worship of Him has not become real. Therefore, I challenge you to move beyond the stereotypical view of worship and begin to see and understand worship from a biblical perspective.

The parameters of worship as set forth by Jesus are made evident during his encounter with the woman at well:

> Woman, believe me, the hour is coming when neither on this mountain nor in Jerusalem will you worship the Father. <u>You worship what you do not know</u>; we worship what we know, for salvation is from the Jews. <u>But the hour is coming, and is now here, when the true worshipers will worship the Father in spirit and truth</u>, for the Father is seeking such people to worship him.

Beyond Religion

> <u>God is a spirit, and those who worship him must worship in spirit and truth.</u>
>
> – John 4:21-24

From this conversation we are given three distinct characteristics of worship:

1. **Worship is not limited to a location** – "Woman, believe me, the hour is coming when neither on this mountain nor in Jerusalem will you worship the Father."

2. **Our worship must be pure** – "...and those who worship Him must worship in spirit and truth."

3. **True worship moves God on our behalf** – "...for the Father is seeking such people to worship Him.

While taking part in the discussion with the woman at the well, Jesus makes a powerful statement when he says to her, "You worship what you do not know." This has become a distinctive characteristic of believers of this generation who "worship" the worship experience but have yet to honor and reverence God through their obedience.

> This people honors me with their lips, but their heart is far from me; in vain do they worship me, teaching as doctrines the commandments of men.
>
> – Matthew 15:8-9

We have come upon the hour where the Father is looking for true worshippers to appear and if we want to experience a real movement of God in the earth, then our worship of Him must become real. Therefore, worship can no longer be limited to what takes place in our cultured facilities; but it must be what flows from the heart. It cannot be what we offer up to God in the form of our choreographed movements or programmed praise, but there must be a bowing down in the spirit that says to God that we want to live completely surrendered lives before Him; because simply reaching our hands toward heaven becomes an empty gesture if our hearts have not been extended to Him.

As sons and daughters of God we must let go of the building mentality and not get so caught up in what takes place inside of our religious halls. God never intended for man to run from building to building in hopes of chasing down a worship experience because worship is not an experience that anyone can hope to capture. Worship, in its purest form is a lifestyle, and not just any lifestyle, but one that seeks to honor God.

For too long, worship has been limited to the events that take place during our Sunday morning service and consequently, our worship ends at the culmination of every "good" service. However, if, when service concludes, we are not moved toward a more sincere obedience, then we have not truly honored the King. Worship is only real when it leads us closer to the will of God.

"Worship is only real when it leads us into the will of God"

God is listening for a certain sound to ring out in the earth but that sound is not the sound of music. God wants to hear is His heart beating through every one of His sons and daughter in the earth. Therefore, it is my earnest prayer that the heartbeat of heaven will echo in the ears of this generation so that we will know the heart of the Father and carry out His will in the earth. And so as we stand here, on the precipice of truth, we have a major decision to make. Do we carry on with our pagan styles of worship – honoring the traditions of our fathers or do we completely submit to the will of God – even if it means us leaving the church.

God is preparing to birth something new into the earth but what He is birthing is not coming out of our local assemblies – it is coming from you and me. The Father is gathering a remnant of worshippers and He is pushing them outside of the fortified walls of the church building for the advancement of His Kingdom in the earth. There is an army being raised among this generation – a movement of God's people dedicated to protecting the integrity of the Kingdom and defending its principles against the influences of this world.

Up until now, the whole creation has eagerly been

awaiting the manifestation of the sons and daughters of God **(Romans 8:19)** and we are who they have been looking for. We are the army that is being raised in this age and we have been positioned in the earth, for such a time as this; to reflect the glory of the Father and to advance His Kingdom in the earth. And so once again God is calling forth children – those who have His heart and He is re-establishing us in our rightful position of authority. By reinstating man as a legal authority in the earth, God is looking to once again rule in the earth through us.

"**God wants to rule earth's territory through you!**"
PURPOSED FOR THE EARTH

We must understand that God never created man with the intentions of taking him to heaven. Man was created for the sole purpose of inheriting ruler-ship of the earth; to colonize it and bring it under his control. From the very beginning, it was the Father's will to have the culture of heaven invade the earth through His created sons and daughters. This was the initial feat that God tried to accomplish through Adam and Eve but after they failed; it was carried over and crafted into the life of Jesus which he made this apparent in His teaching on prayer.

> And when you pray, do not heap up empty phrases as the Gentiles do, for they think they will be heard for their many words. Do not be like them, for your Father knows what you

> need before you ask him. Pray then like this: Our Father in heaven, hallowed be your name. <u>Your kingdom come, your will be done, on earth as it is in heaven…</u>
>
> – Matthew 6:9-10

Bringing the culture of heaven to the earth is the responsibility of everyone living under the influence of God's Kingdom and whether we do this as a unified front or it results in us fulfilling our individual destinies; all of our efforts should be directed toward seeing the will of God done in the earth as it is in heaven. But as religion continues to affect how we operate in the earth, the dominion factor ceases to be a focal point of our existence because it is continuously being eclipsed by man's misconception of heaven.

It is because heaven has been introduced into our lives from a religious standpoint that we have completely abandoned our responsibility to the earth and, instead, have taken on an escapism mentality which has led many to believe that heaven is God's ultimate goal for humanity. However, escapism from the earth is not a biblical concept nor will you find it evident in any of the teachings of Jesus. In fact, the bible says that:

> The heavens are the Lord's heavens, but the earth he has given to the children of man.
>
> – Psalms 115:16

> And they sang a new song, saying 'Worthy are you to take the scroll and to open its seals for you were slain, and by your blood you ransomed people for God from every tribe and language and people and nation, and <u>you have made them a kingdom and priests to our God, and they shall reign on the earth</u>.
>
> – Revelation 5:9-10

Therefore man's ultimate reality – the purpose given to him by God – was not to have man escape the earth with the hopes of obtaining heaven; but to have man impact the earth on heaven's behalf. And so we who are truly striving to live according to purpose; we must understand that we cannot even begin to put our hope towards heaven until we have committed ourselves to living out our responsibility in the earth.

"God never meant for man to escape the earth; but to empower us to impact it on his behalf."

Jesus, while anticipating his pending death, spent a great deal of time praying for his disciples. And in what could be considered one of his most heartfelt prayers, Jesus never asks for the disciples be taken out of this world. His only request was that the Father would protect them while they were still in it.

> <u>I do not ask that you take them out of the world</u>, but that you keep them

> from the evil one. They are not of the world, just as I am not of the world. Sanctify them in truth; your word is truth. <u>As you have sent me into the world, so I have sent them into the world</u>. And for their sake I consecrate myself, that they also may be sanctified in truth.
>
> – John 17:15-19

We must understand that we have been set in the earth because this is where our purpose lies. If God, the Creator of heaven and earth, wanted us in heaven, He would have put us there. Instead, He placed us in earth for the purpose of colonization and Kingdom expansion; which makes Paul's claim that we are ambassadors of Christ **(II Corinthians 5:20)** one that we should all seek to understand, if we are to take on a kingdom mindset.

An ambassador by definition is a diplomatic representative sent from his or her country of origin to represent the interest of his government in foreign territory. Ambassadors do not have their own agendas nor do they speak their own mind; but they operate on behalf of the governments they represent. Ambassadors are not subject to the laws of the foreign land they are in but are free to conduct themselves according to the laws and mandates of their own government.

As children of God and joint heirs to the throne,

we have been sanctioned in the earth as ambassadors to the Kingdom of God. In our role as ambassadors we represent the interest of our King in the earth realm, which means that we are not subject to the laws of this world or any other governmental system that operates in opposition to the Kingdom of God. Therefore, we must take up our mantle of authority and begin to operate in the earth under the seal of our King for the purpose of subduing the earth and expanding the Kingdom on His behalf.

> And God blessed them. And God said to them "Be fruitful and multiply and fill the earth and subdue it...
>
> – Genesis 1:28

Because we represent the Kingdom, it is important for us to understand that whenever a king wanted to relay an urgent message to a foreign dignitary, he did not just send anyone. He would send his heir, thereby, signifying the importance of the message being sent. In return, the heir would undertake the role of ambassador; representing the interest of his father in a foreign land while exercising full authority of the kingdom. Jesus is the perfect example of an heir turned ambassador: He was sent from heaven (the kingdom of His Father) with and urgent message (the gospel of the kingdom) to a foreign nation (the world). He came with the full the authority of heaven to extend to God's people in the earth full citizenship in to the Kingdom of God and the right to be called sons and daughters of the Most High.

We were created to share in the inheritance of the Kingdom as joint heirs with Christ. As joint heirs to the kingdom we also share in the responsibility of extending the Kingdom to the rest of the world. But because we get so caught up in asking God to enlarge our personal space, we fail to realize that the more territory we gain for the King, the greater our inheritance will be once we inherit ruler-ship of the Kingdom.

> And you have caused them to become a Kingdom of priests for our God. And they will reign in the earth.
>
> – Revelations 5:10 NLT

"We will reign in the earth."

As we bring this chapter to a close I want to share with you a letter I wrote to my Facebook friends a little over a year ago. This letter was written with the hopes of inspiring a generation to live according their purpose and today I find it only fitting that I try to inspire you to walk in the authority given you and live according to what you were purposed for in the earth.

Erik L. Cox

The Appeal of an Ambassador

September 9, 2012

Dear sons and daughters of God:

I greet you with the agape` love of Christ and all humbleness of heart – knowing that this is the greatest expression of God's love. This letter is written to you with a great sense of urgency; understanding the need to advance the kingdom of God without delay and causing the earth to resemble and reflect heaven's glory.

We are living in desperate times and the whole creation is groaning, waiting on the manifestation of the sons and daughters of God. Therefore, a remnant of worshippers MUST arise out of this generation – a people not ashamed to stand with boldness on the principles of God's Word. People not divided by religion but a people of a pure heart, who sincerely desire to see the will of our King done in the earth. People determined to honor God through their obedience and their willingness to surrender their lives for His purpose and His Glory – No Conforming. No Adapting. No Excuses. No Compromise.

And so I am writing to encourage you to become that people – people who are willing to walk away from religion so that you may seek the heart of the King and receive the mind of Christ. God is raising an army and He is arming His people with a desire

Beyond Religion

for His Presence, because it is only when we are covered in Him that we can take Him to the nations. So my prayer is that all who receive this letter will position yourselves in the presence of God and allow Him to speak directly to your spirit. We must began to separate ourselves from any and every distraction – including the church – and allow the Father to speak to our hearts.

We must saturate the earth with His Presence by becoming the heartbeat of heaven and we must be so loudly against the earth's core that it awakens this generation to the love of the Father, causing them to seek intimacy with the King. Let the glory of the Lord rise among us and create a culture that causes our territories to resemble heaven. The Father wants this generation to demonstrate His love on the earth.

And so I pray that as you stand unwavering in your faith that God will continue to smile on you and that He will bless you according to His riches in glory. I love you with the heart of the King and stand with you as we expand His kingdom together.

Your Brother in Christ
Erik L. Cox

Erik L. Cox

KINGDOM TRUTHS

- Worship, in its purest form, does not manifest in a song and dance, but it is a lifestyle that seeks to honor God.

- God never meant to have man escape his responsibility to the earth; but to empower us to live according to his purpose.

- Because we share in the inheritance of the Kingdom of God as joint heirs with Christ; we also share in the responsibility of extending the Kingdom to the rest of the world.

- Bringing the culture of heaven to the earth is the responsibility of everyone living under the influence of the Kingdom.

- God wants to rule earth's territory through YOU!!!

CHAPTER SIX
Finding your Faith

"Faith consists in believing when it is beyond the power of reason to believe. – Myles Munroe

IF YOU ARE still turning the pages of this book; unrelenting in your determination to find truth – then let me to be the first to applaud your faith. We have already accomplished a great deal and are forging ahead with remarkable progress. The first five chapters have allowed us to explore some key aspects of the Kingdom of God while helping us to discover our individual purposes and unearth our true identities; all of which are critical elements in our quest to become who we were created to be. But now that we have come to the end of our journey, there is one more element that MUST be discussed in order to make this journey complete and this element is FAITH.

Now we all talk a pretty good game when it comes to this thing called faith, needless to say, everyone believes they have it. Yet, there is one fundamental principle always operating in the Kingdom of God and this principle reminds us, that, without faith it is impossible to please God **(Hebrews 11:6).** And since we fail to understand faith from a spiritual point of view, many of us have a shallow understanding of what our purpose is, and as a result, we are unable operate in our God-given authority. And without a working definition of faith we are incapable of reaching our full potential in God and, consequently, we will only be allowed to get but so far in in the Kingdom of God.

Faith, then, is the key that unlocks every door within the Kingdom of God and puts the resources of heaven at our full disposal in the earth. Think about it! When Peter faithfully acknowledged Jesus as the Christ, the Son of the Living God; it is possible that he could have been given anything. Yet, out of all the things that he could have been given, Jesus specifically gave to him the keys to the Kingdom (knowledge of the Kingdom) and the power to bind and loose in the earth. But why was this?

Keys (knowledge) represent authority (power), hence, we have the phrase, "knowledge is power." And by giving Peter keys to the Kingdom, Jesus was empowering him to operate in the earth as God operates in heaven. So it happens to be, that, whenever the Father entrusts one of His created sons and daughters with keys (knowledge) to the Kingdom; there is an expectation for us to operate in the fullness of His power so that we can unlock the mysteries of the kingdom to the rest of the world. However, it takes great faith on our part, to maneuver in the earth with the mindset of God and know that all of heaven is at our beck and call. It takes even greater faith to be able to take on the characteristics of God and accept that we were created with god-like capabilities for the sole purpose of exercising dominion in the earth.

This is why our faith in God cannot be circumstantial. It is not enough for us to say that we trust God when it comes to acquiring the materialistic, mundane things of the world if we are not going to offer Him that same trust when it comes to living out His will in the earth. True faith, then, has nothing to do with the acquisition of things; but has everything to do with walking in the freedom of who we are. And if faith has been instituted into our lives so that we could become what we were created to be from the foundations of the world, then we must evaluate where we are spiritually and begin to question why we are unable to demonstrate the power of God, when it has been readily available for our use.

Now my personal guess would be that ever since God has been introduced into our lives from a religious perspective, our identities in Him have been stolen; leaving us to operate in the earth as only replicas of our former selves. Furthermore, because biblical truths are constantly being altered to fit man's personal beliefs, religion as a whole has become nothing but a tool of pacification; keeping us content with who we are so that we will never seek the truth concerning who we were called to be. But how did we get here in the first place? How did we go from having dominion over the earth to being dominated in the earth? How did we go from being created in the image and likeness of God to believing that we are nothing more than sinners saved by grace? How did we go from having god-like capabilities to accepting peasant-like conditions? And if the bible is the authentic Word of God and every word of God proves true **(Proverbs 30:5);** how did we go from advancing the will of God in the earth to propagating a religious belief, pledging our allegiance to a system that identifies with Christ in name but has nothing to do with Christ in nature?

Almost immediately after birth, we are submersed into religion and bombarded with all types of spiritual concepts and religious ideas that have nothing to do with God's purpose for our lives. Because these ideas are constantly being engrained into our way of thinking, they have single-handedly been used to shape our entire belief system. As a result, we are afraid to entertain any idea outside of the scope of our religious views because it is much easier to accept what we are told to be rather than taking the initiative to discover who we actually are. But today I offer you the opportunity to take back your identity and pick up the mantle of authority given to you at creation by simply suggesting to you that we were created to be "god" in the earth.

Now I understand that by making such a bold claim, I take the risk of rattling someone's faith. And even though the claim, itself, can be supported scripturally; many will still question its authenticity –

Beyond Religion

all too eager to disregard its truth, simply because it is not something that is taught inside of their Christianity. Yet, I encourage all of you to keep reading and not to be afraid to grab hold of who you were created to be, because contrary to the ideas that have been embedded in us through the rudimentary teachings of the pulpit preacher; we were never created to serve a religious purpose. We were specifically chosen by God to embody His Spirit, His essence, and His being for the purpose of exercising dominion in the earth. And as the embodiment of God in the earth, the goal for us was never religion. But by handcrafting us in His image and likeness, God was giving us son-ship so that we could inherit ruler-ship and become His very heartbeat in the earth.

> I have said, 'Ye are gods; and all of you are children of the Most High.
>
> – Psalms 82:6

NOW STOP. INHALE. AND BREATH. I know that this has been a lot take in, but opening your eyes to these truths will prove to be, both, beneficial and necessary if we hope to live as God intended for us to live in the earth. So if you wouldn't mind I going to ask you do something for me. I want you to forget every form of doctrine that has been taught to you up until this now. Just for a moment, I need you to lay aside every religious concept, every pulpit principle, and every church idea that has ever come into your hearing because if I am going to get you to embrace the "god" in you; then it cannot be done based on someone else's interpretation of biblical concepts. It would be expedient, then, for us to exercise a certain level of faith in this matter and allow that faith to lead us outside of the walls of the church until we are forced us to seek an authentic view of God which is solely based on biblical truths.

At some point we will be held accountable for all the things that we have allowed to come into our lives and shape our faith, therefore, it is in our best interest to challenge everything that comes into our hearing so that we can gain an accurate understanding of biblical concepts for ourselves, because every day our faith is constantly being developed by the things that we hear.

> So then faith cometh by hearing, and
> hearing by the word of God.
> – Romans 10:17

And so if the development of our faith is directly connected to the things that we hear, it's no wonder why we reject the notion that we were created to be "god" in the earth – it's simply not something that we hear every day. For too long we have allowed men and women with self-given titles to freely speak into our lives, often internalizing their words as if they are spoken directly from the mouth of God. But the disappointing reality that we will soon be faced with – those who decide to seek biblical truth for themselves – is that most of the things that are being handed down to us from our pulpits have been pre-programmed into the church's doctrine to teach and are not necessarily truths founded on biblical principles.

Understand that no one has the original words of God. We only have translations, retranslations, mistranslations and man's interpretation. And by taking everything that we hear and digesting it as truth; we leave no room for ourselves to process the Word of God as it was written. This makes it spiritually irresponsible to shrug off any idea that doesn't coincide man's Christianity as false doctrine, when we ourselves, have not committed to seeking truth beyond our own religion. And to reject everything outside of our religious beliefs without obtaining knowledge, we force ourselves to walk outside on our own destinies.

So let's come back to our original idea; the point that I have been trying to make since the opening of this chapter – actually since the start of this book. This idea highlights a truth that has been left hidden inside the Word of God and overshadowed by our religious beliefs – beliefs that we then passed down from generation to generation until the people of God in the earth no longer identified with the original intent of God. In this book I have tried to unmask God's plan for our lives by introducing kingdom concepts and communicating the reason why we created in His image and likeness.

But how do you keep a slave a slave? By reinforcing into him the idea that he is a slave, because as stated earlier, the things that we believe is often shaped by the things that we hear. With this in mind, the question becomes how do you free a slave? You free a slave by getting him to believe that he was created for something far greater than slavery, and when this idea has been firmly planted, he will choose for himself the right time to rise up and revolt against the system that has kept him enslaved him for so long. In the same manner, if we are to free God's people from the religious system that has enslaved generations of believers, we must first reinforce to them the idea that they were created to be a reflection of God in the earth.

The first thing we were given at creation was the image and likeness of God. And if, the genetic makeup of our biological fathers determines how we are identified ethnically in the earth, then why is it considered blasphemy for us to identify ourselves as "gods" when the bloodline of our spiritual Father is GOD by nature. And so my question is, "Who raped you of your identity?" Who made it okay for us to identify ourselves with titles and to classify ourselves by our denomination affiliations? Who told you were Baptist, Methodist, Evangelical, or Pentecostal? Who called you into apostleship or elected you bishop and overseer to God's people? Who told you that your place in ministry was to sing in the choir, usher on the usher board, or to be on the board? I can say with upmost certainty that Jesus didn't. And if Jesus didn't do it, why are we doing it?

Every day we try to communicate to the world that we are followers of Christ, yet, most of the things that we do inside of our religious systems are in fact anti-Christ. Show me in the written word, any instance, where Jesus supported denominationalism. Where he handed out ministry specifications and church job descriptions or promoted a particular belief. Show me in the word, any one time, where Jesus applauded the religious efforts of man and I'll show you in that same word where he referenced man as "god."

> [And] Jesus answered them, "Is it not written in your law, 'I said, you are gods?' And if he called them gods to whom the word came – <u>and if Scripture cannot be broken</u> – why do you say of him whom the Father consecrated and sent into the world, 'You are blaspheming, 'because I said, 'I am the Son of God?'
>
> – John 10:36

It is important that we recognize that we are living in some of the most critical times in this era of human history, and either the Word of God will be used to promote a truth or it will be used to keep us in bondage. And so as I introduce this concept of us being "god" in the earth into your spirit; know that I do so with the greatest concern for your spiritual well-being. As sons and daughters of God we should be living as God purposed us to live. And if Jesus said that we would do "greater works" in the earth, yet, we remain powerless in our efforts to change the very conditions we live in; then there is something seriously wrong with how we are applying His Word to our lives.

Now that we have reached the end of the road of this very informative journey, I would never ask you to take any of my words at face value. You would be a fool to do such a thing. I simply ask that you will start being accountable for your own spiritual growth and take time to read the Word of God from cover to cover, so that you can determine what truth is for yourself. See the Word of God was written; uncorrupted by man's personal opinions and individual biases. Allow it to speak directly to your spirit and let your faith take you on a journey that leads you outside of the restricted areas of religion and into the original idea of God.

God's image and likeness, this was God's original plan for mankind and it is still your current reality. We were created for dominion and ruler-ship in the earth and I say this, not as one coerced by doctrine but as one who has truly sought what it means to be created in the image and likeness of God. And if you are still skeptical concerning this truth note this: The

Beyond Religion

Bible begins with us ruling and having authority and the Bible ends with us doing the same.

> Then God said, "Let us make man in our image, after our likeness. **And let them have dominion** over the fish of the sea and over the birds of the heavens and over the livestock **and over all the earth** and over every creeping thing that creeps on the earth.
>
> – Genesis 1:26
>
> And they sang a new song, saying, "Worthy are you to take the scroll and to open it seals, for you were slain, and by your blood your ransomed people for God from every tribe and language and people and nation, and you have made them a kingdom and priest to our God, **and they shall reign on the earth.**
>
> – Revelations 5:9-10

WE ARE THE HEARTBEAT OF GOD IN THE EARTH!!!

Erik L. Cox

KINGDOM TRUTHS

- Keys represent authority and when God gives His children knowledge of the kingdom, there is an expectation that we will unlock the mysteries of the kingdom to his people in the earth.

- Our faith in God cannot be circumstantial, therefore it cannot be based on the conditions surrounding our circumstances.

- We were created in the image and likeness of God so that we can become His very heartbeat in the earth.

- Religion has stolen our true identities and has been used a tool of pacification, to keep us from seeking who we were truly created to be.

- The Bible begins with us ruling on behalf of God. And the Bible ends with us ruling with God.

ABOUT THE AUTHOR

Former assistant pastor under the leadership of Rev. Horace L. Sheffield, III and former host of "Religion on the Line" on 1440 WDRJ; and while serving as praise team leader for People of the Light Ministries and New Galilee Missionary Baptist Church; Erik Cox decided to walk away from it all in order to find truth.

This search for truth led him outside of the walls of the modern day assembly and into the path of Min. Darrie Williams, who he now embraces as a brother and colleague in a joint effort to expand the Kingdom of God and together they are preparing for one of the greatest evangelistic movements of our time, so that the heart of heaven will invade the earth through the hearts of God's chosen sons and the daughters.

Erik believes that God's people were created to reflect the glory of the Father in the earth and the only way to do this effectively is by coming outside of our buildings and taking the heart of God to the people of God and he has left the comforts of pulpit preaching to go into the wilderness of Detroit and offer a broken people God's heart.

Under the Kingdom Expansion Project, a movement

spearheaded by Darrie Williams with Erik sharing in leadership responsibilities; people are receiving prayer on the streets and souls are accepting Jesus as Lord. Homeless people are being fed and bound people are being delivered and set free. Erik's philosophy is simply:

> "At the end of the day, it matters not who I am. What matters is whose I am and when His people see me operating in His power, then I have just won another victory for the King and His Kingdom; and this is what it's all about – expanding territory for the King."

www.ingramcontent.com/pod-product-compliance
Lightning Source LLC
Chambersburg PA
CBHW032140040426
42449CB00005B/330